LIVING
AS
GOD

LIVING
AS
GOD

Healing the Separation

P. RAYMOND STEWART

Namaste Publishing

VANCOUVER, CANADA

Library and Archives Canadian Cataloguing in Publication Data

Stewart, P. Raymond
   Living as God: healing the separation / P. Raymond Stewart.

   Includes bibliographical references.

   ISBN 0-9736512-0-2

   1. God. 2. Spiritual life. I Title.
   BT165.S72 2004 202.117 C2004-906093-7

Published in Canada by
NAMASTE PUBLISHING
P.O. Box 62084
Vancouver, British Columbia, v6J 4A3
www.namastepublishing.com
E-mail: Namaste@telus.net

Distributed in Canada by Dempsey
Distributed in USA by New Leaf Distributors and DeVorss & Company
Printed and bound in Canada by Friesens

This book is dedicated to the one holding it now.

CONTENTS

DEDICATION

Yes, this is for you. You didn't come across these words by accident. Nothing ever happens by accident. What is occurring in your life right now is deliberate. The whole universe has conspired to create this moment exactly the way it is. Together, we have chosen to come to this page.

I have chosen it.

You have chosen it.

We have chosen it.

For all of life is connected: each breath and subtle movement influences all that is.

And together we are One.

How you choose to respond to this book influences the fate of the world. You are the only part of the collective whole who can alter the part of us that is you.

Your life is holy. This book has come to remind you of that. In fact, the whole universe exists to remind you of your true worth, to remind you that you are immeasurably more than a separate little person.

So I, a part of you, devote this book to you who is a part of me. This part of the One Self is dedicated to bringing forth whatever can help you more fully experience the joy and beauty of life.

This is your request.

This is your answer—sent forth with and from Love.

This book is dedicated to you: the One
Holding
        this Now.

WORDS

Once upon a time, when we had an inner certainty of the truth of our Being, we didn't need words for guidance. And so may it be again. Words offer a poor path to the reality of the ineffable, but for now they are still one of the few tools for sharing ideas, feelings, and experiences related to the spiritual realm. Humankind has called this realm many things: the Tao, the Void, the Rigpa, God, Source. On and on go the words that are used in an attempt to express that which lies beyond their limitations. The Infinite cannot be contained in a word any more than your essence can be conveyed by your name.

When it comes to words, the vast majority of humanity still associates a state of ultimate peace and fulfillment with the word "God". Consequently, this is the most highly charged of all words. It carries every confused vision, every misconception, yet every cherished hope of mankind. Because of this, an evolutionary clarification of "God" is needed.

We say the grandest expression of man is godliness. This is the pinnacle of our human potential. But most neither know godliness nor how to express it.

Our greatest human yearning remains our need to know God. This book is brought into manifestation by the collective call for help in this search. In our search, we must be ready to go beyond the word "God" and what we currently associate with it. This is the journey we are about to take. Words can still serve us in this journey, as long as we do not mistake these aids, these pointers to Truth, for Truth itself.

Is God outside of you, inside of you, or all around you? Is God a person or a power? A fantasy or a reality? God may mean ultimate power for you. God may be a name for nothingness, as in some Buddhist texts. God is represented by a single man for some Christians, every man for the Hindus, silence for the Taoists, and sound to the Vedic seers. God evokes a state of peace to some, and to others God is a legitimate reason for war. God has been described as a powerful lion of a creator, and also as meek as a lamb. The planet earth is God for the aboriginal Americans, and everything *but* the physical realm is God for some New Age Thinkers. The Tantrists find God through sex, yet Catholic priests seek God through chastity. Why such confusion? Why such disagreement?

In truth, all are correct. God is without opposite or opposition. God is the manifest universe and also the infinite unmanifest potential of all life. God is exempt from nothing and indeed excludes Itself from nothing. Not for any reason. Not ever.

How can we remove the encrusted, disfigured outer shell of the word "God" so as to reveal its innermost truth? If we could fully convey the complete, indisputable truth of this one word, then in publishing it to the world, all seeking and suffering would cease. This is the dauntless challenge and intent of this book. If it is achieved in you, it will not be because of the words, but because of your readiness to *feel* the truth to which they point. Awareness comes not through the thoughts that words evoke. Awareness is a *felt* experience that leaves a new, true, and permanent change in perception of reality—of what is so. It is the hungry mind that wants to reduce the ineffable to the confines of logical reasoning. The thinking mind separates out; it cannot conceive of wholeness and thereby interferes with truly experiencing awareness of the One Self.

As you read, you may arrive at the bottom of a page and realize that although you have understood what is written, you cannot actually recall a single sentence. This is truly good news. It means that you are releasing the limitations of thought, of the thinking mind, and are being carried by the higher vibration of the heart that is embedded between these words and lines. This is the aim of all true teachers, whether they take the form of a human or a book. For any thought is useful only to the degree that it leads us into a deeper awareness through *feeling*. So do not rush through this work with a hungry mind. Let it sink in deeply. Let its feeling-tone linger in your energy field. If you do, it will speak to you and reach you on many levels in perfect, harmonious ways.

We say God, Goddess, All That Is, the Self, Consciousness, Energy, Being, Mahatma, Yahweh, Jehovah, Rigpa, I Am Presence, the Void, Isness, Oneness, Spirit, Tao, You, Me, Love, Light, Us, We, I, He, Her, It, One Self—and always these words point to God. Indeed, we are all synonymous: each of us has the same essential nature. If we understand one person fully or the essence behind one name of Spirit truly, we understand them all.

"God" is the word we use most often to describe all that we do *not* understand. Yet it is also the word for all that we *do* understand. But once we think we understand something, we stop calling it God. We used to call a flash of light from the sky a sign of God, but now we know it simply as lightning. At one time, saving someone from dying of a poison would have been called a miracle. Now, with medical antidotes, we can achieve a quick chemical response to the poison rendering it non-lethal to the body. The more we seem to understand, the less we need to ascribe to God. From this perspective, God has become increasingly narrow in some people's minds. However, when we start to sense the Spirit of all things—the essence behind each form—we find that the word "God" expands again to encompass everything.

For centuries, most of humanity has held an extremely dysfunctional image of an outside, anthropomorphic God, which has severely limited the human race in all its endeavors and been the cause of much suffering. In order to break free, to evolve, this conditioned, misleading view must be dropped. Yes, we could try to simply avoid the word "God" in our philosophical dialogues and spiritual pursuits, yet eventually it must be integrated for our own inner healing. We can talk about Universal Life Force or the Universal Mind, but eventually our inner self will ask, "But how does all of this relate to God?" That is the fundamental question.

A requisite part of this inquiry is how do *you* relate to God? When you close your eyes and are still, and say the word "God", what images or thoughts emerge? What does God mean for *you*? Do you feel anger towards God, fearful of Him, or do you feel ambivalent, as if the word were merely a symbol of a vague unseen power? Do you feel love towards Her, or do you feel neglected?

Regardless of your response, you must someday explore this relationship, for your path to inner peace spirals through its essence.

Let us finally resolve all issues that stand between us and our world, between you and your family, between you and your self, between you and me, between you and God. You have brought this book to yourself now so that these words may break down the long-standing walls of self-imposed separation, thereby enabling you to experience again the peace that comes through unity with God.

Since we command that which we truly understand, are you ready to reclaim the power in your life? That is why we are here. Life, God, wants to extend Itself, and It does so through you. This is our individual and collective purpose—to give expression to God, to be the Living God. It is through us that God can come to know Its Self. And this includes you. Through our existence, God can look on Its Self and see Its beauty.

2

THE FIRST WORD

"In the beginning was the Word, and the Word was with God, and the Word was God." (John 1:1) Then the Word was dispersed and made flesh, and could relate within Its Self. And in doing so, space and time were born. With space came distance. Separation was perceived. And with time, that separation was believed, and God became estranged within Its Self. The first Word, the One Word, had appeared to become the many, and the out breath was complete.

The mystery of the first line of the Gospel of John has perplexed many for centuries. It has left readers of the Bible wondering, "What *is* this Word?" Yet at the time this was written, its meaning was not obscure. The phrase "the Word" was borrowed from earlier, widely known Vedic texts, where it was often used as a direct substitute for their holiest of all words, the "Aum" or "Om", which is considered to be the word that represents all life. Translated into English, the word is notably similar: "Am", or more commonly, "I Am". The New Testament simply follows this tradition of substitution.

Therefore, whenever we see "the Word", we know that this implies the holy name of God: "I Am". So, in more modern language, this earlier quotation reads: "In the beginning was the I Am, and the I Am was with God, and the I Am was God." The word *of* God, and the word *for* God, and the *name* of God are all the same thing— the I Am. I Am = God. The I Am *is* God. How many of us, however, pause to note and explore the obvious connection we have with this name of God? For is it not our name as well? This speaks of our mystical connection.

It has been over 2000 years since Jesus walked the earth, preaching the kingdom of heaven within. Since then, His words, the word "God", and the word *of* God have been altered significantly. We are ready now for an evolutionary leap in consciousness which will bring clarity and unity to all spiritual teachings. It is time to redeem the words of God. For that is the purpose of the Christ—to bring God to life in the hearts of all men. It is time to redeem the word "God". That has been the mission of every true spiritual master—to make God live again among men, to resurrect man's Holy Spirit to breathe the life of remembrance into our consciousness. In order to do this, it is necessary to reject any part of your self that feels in essence different from and potentially less than the man known as Jesus. This is true for any spiritual guide you look up to, be it Jesus, Buddha, Mohammed, Archangel Michael, or Saint Germain. Although this may be against the teachings of established Christian religions, it is a glorious irony that it is exactly what Jesus Himself did teach: "The works that I do you will also do, and greater works than these you will do."

(John 14:12) Do not believe that you will only do these things when you get to heaven, for He also said, "The kingdom of heaven is here and now." (Matthew 4:17) It is indeed ironic that what some would have us believe is the greatest sin is, in fact, not sin at all, but a sign— a sign that we are remembering the truth: we and God are One.

This is what we have come here to remember—I Am that "I Am." The great teachings implore us to "Know thy self." They also tell us to "Know thy God." However, most importantly, they tell us that to know thy self *is* to know God. Although we may perceive this to be most radical, it is truly the most primal of spiritual teachings. This message has never changed, nor will it ever. Humanity's acceptance of it is the only thing to ever shift.

Jesus understood clearly his connection between himself and the Father. That is the source of his power and powerful influence on the world. He had power because he lived in constant awareness of and alignment with his oneness with the Father, with Divine Source. To worship Jesus the man or any other spiritual master or prophet is to gravely miss the mark. Do not worship their physical form or worship them for their works; recognize instead the very same glory residing in your own self. That is what the Buddha taught us to do. That is what Jesus taught us was possible. Yet their teachings have been skewed and clouded. That is why we are now calling forth other aspects of the One Self to express again the eternal truth for which we thirst. This book comes to remind you that you, as part of the One Self, are God.

You are God. This is the obvious truth we do not hear, clearly expressed and demonstrated by masters we have ignored. God being love extends Itself naturally to create All That Is. This is the great insight we prevent ourselves from having, going as far as creating institutions and religions to keep us from seeing it. Why? Because to accept this truth would mean the death of all we have been conditioned to believe. It would mean the end of our current perception of who we have come to see our selves as—separate, vulnerable, limited persons needing to struggle and defend ourselves against "others" to exist. There would be no more conflict, no more aggression, no more drama, no more unease, displeasure, or even disease if we were to accept our Oneness—our Oneness as God. Does this sound like heaven? Certainly not to the ego. To the ego, to the false-created self that is based on separation from others, it means death. And that is why people tend to unconsciously resist the purest spiritual teachings which have been with us for centuries: they do not serve the needs or goals of the egoic mind. The full realization of the One Self is, indeed, a death. It is the death of that separate, projected self that most people believe to be their whole being. It is this belief in separation which prevents their spiritual surrender.

It is of little benefit merely to repeat to yourself that Krishna lives in every heart, that Buddha is alive in everything, that the Tao flows with and through all things. Each time we point to the same truth. But do we truly *hear* it? Will we *hear* it if we make it personal? Doesn't saying, "I am God" change everything? How do you feel when you think of it? Dare you even say it out loud? There is enormous resistance to this thought in the human psyche. It can bring great fear. For it changes *everything.*

We have said that we need and desire great changes in our world. And we have heard and answered our prayers. For the first time in human history, there appear to be enough individuals who have the readiness and level of awareness to make these changes. These individuals know that we cannot change just a little bit. We must be transformed. And our transformation occurs through complete acceptance of and surrender to the Spirit in and behind all things.

3

WHO AM I?

Who am I? This is the most natural and fundamental of all inquiries. God already answered when asked this question. She responded, "I Am that I Am." And we questioned God's answer. "What does this mean?" we wondered. "What is this I Am?" "Who is this I Am?" We tried to give *form* to the answer.

"Who am I?" Always, we come back to the same question. But who are we really asking? Ourself? God? More importantly, who is it who responds? Always, this question has been in the first person. Who Am I? I Am that I Am. This question and this answer are always the same—regardless of who is asking it, regardless of who is responding to it. It is no different for one person than it is for another. The question and answer will be the same whether we ask God, whether we ask another being, or even if God asks us. But this still leaves us wondering: Who are You, God? That is what we *really* want to know.

We say we are soul searching, that we are trying to find our self, and that we are looking for God. Yet these all involve the same process—the inquiry into the nature of our Source. Finding this Source is what great saints identify as the purpose of life. Different descriptions of and approaches to finding the purpose of life fill many books. One Eastern spiritual tradition simply and clearly called the paths and the goal 'self-realization'.

It is significant that past and current spiritual masters tell us that to know thy self is also to know God. However, this has been difficult for us to comprehend. How can it be that we are one and the same? And if we are, what does this *really* mean? This is what we are here to clarify: Who and What is the I Am?

Listen. I Am in the silence between these words and lines, and underneath the very air you breathe. What I Am and who you are, are the same. We share our essential Beingness. Every heart beats with the same life force. That is the miracle and mystery of life. Let us explore our essence so that we may come to the *felt* realization that who I truly am and who you truly are, are the same.

4

ABOUT THE AUTHOR

P. Raymond Stewart is a pseudonym, simply a label. The author's name does not matter. It could be any name—Chris, Raymond, Pauline, or your name, if you like. Every name belongs to both you and me, for we are each part of everyone. The heart that speaks here is the same one that is deep within you and everyone else. Also, the physical identity of the person who birthed this book does not matter. It is truly irrelevant whether a man or a woman, a Caucasian or an Asian, a scholar or a priest put this to paper. All that matters is that this book *is*.

Be willing to suspend your belief that a single author wrote this book. Instead, be open to the possibility, to the realization that we all are One and therefore it has taken the agreement of the whole universe to get this book into your hands. This, like any book or any thing, is the perfect expression of one part of us with the agreement of and for the benefit of the other parts of us.

We all agreed that this book be written. And here it is.

5

INTRODUCTION

Let me introduce you to God.

He is right here, standing with you. She is right now hearing you, feeling you. God is always with us, as we've been told. So where is She? Why can't we experience Him for ourselves? Simply because we do not recognize God.

You know not who you are. Go now, and look in the mirror. Look behind the familiar form. Do you see who is looking back at you from behind those beautiful eyes? This is the God you do not recognize, for It looks surprisingly just like you! Now, go and look at a neighbour. Do you see who is looking back at you from behind those beautiful eyes? This is the God that you do not recognize, for It looks surprisingly just like your neighbour Tom!

Both of you, and everything that is, are united as a single field of consciousness. Simultaneously, we are also dispersed into many points of experience, where our name could be Peter, or Jesus, or Maryanne. If we have forgotten this, it is all right. We have allowed ourselves to forget. We can also allow ourselves to remember. It is as simple as this.

6

WHEN THE LEAST IS THE MOST

Me is not the One who is great.

It is the One Spirit, as *me that is great.*

It is a great error to believe that *I* could possibly be better than *you*. Indeed, this is truly impossible. At the level of essence, at the spiritual level, we are all equal. For this reason, all self-realized beings are very humble. If you feel in any way that you are greater than or less than another, this is a sure indication that you are not seeing with correct vision. You are not seeing with the eyes of the Soul.

Pride is the trademark of the ego. True humility is the trademark of the spiritual master. We can't claim to personally own or accomplish anything as a separate person, since all comes from the omniscience and omnipotence of the One Self. This is the realization of the master and why the master is so humble. Therefore, bring humility to all that you do. For humility vanquishes the ego. It dissolves all boundaries. No simple passivity or modesty will do. It must be true humility—the releasing of all thoughts that set you apart from another by claiming you are better than, stronger than, more powerful than another.

True humility occurs when you psychologically let go of everything that you used to think of as your own: ideas, possessions, desires, fears—all attachments are surrendered to the all-inclusiveness of the One. You recognize that all is embodied in the One, the I Am Presence that is All. Releasing pride involves understanding that your personal identity is nothing more than a façade, that you are Divine Presence. Because of this, there is nothing to work towards or try to hold onto, since you are All and embody All. In God consciousness, there is no isolation or comparison. Everything is shared; nothing is hidden since there is nothing that needs to be protected through pretence.

To quickly experience humility, you may want to go do something the mind may find typically embarrassing, and instead of letting it make you shrink and feel inferior, laugh at its inability to touch your true self. Instead, expand into the experience. Next, go and do something grand, magnanimous—anything to try to make yourself look better or stand out from another. Then remind yourself that all of your personal efforts to be morally superior, stronger than, better than others are also in vain. What you think about yourself or what anyone else *thinks* about you could never increase or decrease your true worth.

What could anyone else do that makes him or her more than you are? What could you ever do to make yourself one bit better than your neighbour? In our efforts to be better than we already are and better than others, we only prove how completely we have forgotten something important. We can go beyond nobody. We can only go beyond identifying our selves solely with the body. It is a mistaken belief that needs to be transcended. Identifying solely with our body leads us to believe we are separate. When we let go of all the conditioned mind patterns that speak of separation—of things we need to survive, to succeed, to be happy, to be loved—then the self is finally able to reunite with primal reality. This basic reality to which we return when we release the ego and its ways is the reality in which we are God.

Not *a* god.

The God.

There is only one God, and it is the Oneness.

That One Being lives through every body.

We are not all those things that seem to make us different, separate from others. This superficial layer of self—
the ego—is what prevents us from experiencing our true
nature. We believe we need to grow in consciousness
and become more spiritual to become divine, but this
only gives evidence for and reinforces our belief that we
are separate from God. The limited self-image created
by the ego is what needs to dissolve for the One
Presence to be experienced. It is in stillness that we
become aware of our inner presence, which may be
experienced as personal but is universal. John is not the
one God, yet the one God is within John. For "I Am the
way" not "You are the way."

Who you think you are and your efforts to maintain and enhance that are exactly what keep you from experiencing what you really are—which is already perfect and complete. This message has been difficult to spread. Because the humble—if they choose to speak at all—do not speak loudly, they are often not heard.

Truly, if a hand reaching out of the clouds could point the way best or a person materializing objects out of thin air were truly useful to evoke self-realization, that is what the One Self would use to guide us. However, they are not. These would only reinforce our sense of separation. If a man in white robes appeared from out of the sky to teach us about inner holiness, we might pay attention to his teaching but would end up worshipping him as separate from ourselves. A better way for Spirit to bring peace to earth is for a messenger to grow up in our world as a child, to live as an ordinary human, to blossom into self-realization, and to be an example for others. That is why we have you. This is your spiritual purpose.

It is no mistake that you have humble roots. How else can you meet others on common ground? Your past, filled with mistakes, does not negate your divinity but rather enhances your understanding of and compassion for others and makes you and others more mutually accessible. So do not be hard on yourself for being human.

Identification with the egoic self keeps you from God. The wise soul Sai Baba once put it: "God equals man minus ego." He who is least in ego is most in Spirit. Even if you accept this, you are likely afraid to give up your ego. You see the ego's dissolution as your death since you have been living with the belief that the false egoic self is who you are. Be at peace, though. Death of your true self is impossible. That death cannot come. You cannot lose your true Self: you can only gain remembrance of it. Then you find that what you thought was your self holds but a tiny shred of your magnificence.

The egoic self craves security. The heart insists that moving forward is the only way to real freedom. It is indeed ironic that while we claim we want spiritual enlightenment, we are unwilling to part with our ego identification. It is only the insistence of holding on to this that prevents us from experiencing God. This is what the dramatic tragedies seek to teach us: after the ego has its way—after pride—cometh the fall. To prevent tragedy, relinquish the ego. Surrender to the benevolence of the Oneness. Let pride fall, so it does not fell you. This is the end of human drama—our fictional "stories" born out of perceived separation.

It has been fun to act out our egoic roles, but many have finally had enough. We can choose to stop pretending that we are other than the embodied presence of the One. It is *our* choice—about who *we* are.

End of story.

Beginning of peace.

7

YOU SHALL HAVE
NO OTHER GODS

Within the Oneness, there is no other. The entire cosmos is encoded in every atom. Every reality is a hologram. The microcosm *is* the macrocosm. As above, so below. On earth, as it is in heaven. You contain the whole of life's infinite presence. Your neighbour is part of you, just as is a rock on Mars or the thought of a being light years away. Everything you do, say, or think affects positively or negatively the energies around you and thereby the potential realities of the whole universe. The way a farmer in Thailand chops his food creates a wave in the cosmos that ripples through you as you drive to work. How sensitive you choose to be and how these energies interplay with your own consciousness is up to you.

Keep in mind that what you keep in your mind does truly change the world. For the way that you drive to work influences the way a farmer in Thailand chops his food. Modern physicists refer to this as the 'Butterfly Effect' and tell us of the indisputable evidence of non local cause. This points to our true connection.

Heaven is the experiencing of the One. The portal to it is without door. It is wide enough for all sentient beings to pour through at once. No one is barred; those who do not enter have chosen not to. It is not found after death, nor through some work or more time. Unity is available now. Indeed, it is *only* available right now. It is a decision for complete love.

Mastery is a deceptive word because it carries the notion that we must become more holy in order to be aligned with the One. Godliness, however, may very well be fetching wood and carrying water. It may also be checking out groceries eight hours a day. Every true spiritual master bows to you just as steeply as you do before her, for she sees the divine light in you too. In truth, you cannot accept your own divine light without acknowledging it in your brother.

You will know a master because he is at one with his fellow man. It is true that some holy persons have demonstrated immense power and abundance on earth. Yet it is not their power and abundance that make them holy, but the acceptance of their holiness that allows them to be powerful and experience abundance. To worship a spiritual master as apart from and more worthy than you is idolatry. Those beings are no greater than you. They, like each of us, are simply other facets of the One Self. Mother Mary lives within you. Archangel Michael is an expression of us and so is the stranger on the street. Even the terrorist lives within you. All beings represent different energy frequencies of the One Self.

We have to own and bring to love all facets or our One Self. That of what we call the darkness is God too. If we do not see all as an expression of the One, if we put some in a category by themselves (terrorists, rapists, thieves), we foster separation through projection, making it more difficult for us and for them to transform.

The correct way to see any attack is as a call for inclusion and love that comes from an individual who feels separate and therefore afraid and wanting. And our response should be only one of love. A loving response guarantees that it will be a correct one, meaning it will be most appropriate to the situation and those involved. Our loving response may take the form of soft look, a silent blessing, a helping hand. It could also, however, take the form of mustering up all the loving kindness in our heart, then hitting our attacker over the head. The fierce but compassionate Zen master, in trying to bring more awareness to his beloved students, is an exemplar of this form of love.

Psychics and those who channel are not more gifted than you. They have just experienced that they can tune into different aspects of the One Self, much like we choose to tune into different radio frequencies to hear different programs. Common intuition, novel creations, and breakthrough insights result from nothing other than tapping into the greater intelligence of the One Self. It is for this reason that artists of all kinds, inventors, and the like of Einstein acknowledge a higher "force" at work in what they do or come to see. Synchronicities result from our connection and agreement with other parts of our One Self which influence our denser human plane. See if the more you open to the One Self, the more you experience synchronicities. We also experience this connection with other aspects of our One Self through the aid of what we call angels, through forms of divination such as the Tarot, and through seemingly impossible coincidences.

We are all different beams of the same light – shining into each other, shining through each other. We are all different ways that the same Holy Presence is living and experiencing its one, common light.

You were a master when you were born, when you were growing up, and are a master still. You don't have to *become* holy. You already are. You need only *accept* your holiness. See beyond your seeming imperfections to your perfection. See your divinity even when it is not evident in worldly terms. See the mundane as miraculous. For it is when we are tending to our garden, waiting for the car to be fixed, or buying groceries—when we are fully present and embrace our current expression of the One Self—that we are most divine.

Don't seek yourself outside of yourself. Don't be so eager to be spiritual that you leave your humanity behind. They are the same. *Evolution does not mean giving up human experience in favour of spiritual experience, but means shifting your perception to recognize that the human experience is spiritual.*

All guidance comes from your own self, no matter from whose face or voice it appears to come. It is the One Self that hears your prayers. It is the One Self that answers them.

You speak to yourself when you receive intuitive insights. You speak to yourself when a friend gives loving advice. The voice of the Holy Spirit is one of your many voices. The peace you feel is the peace of your self. The state of grace is your own true state. The love you feel is *you*.

If you have chosen to misperceive yourself in the past, you can choose again. You can now choose to perceive correctly. You can ask your indwelling Holy Spirit to correct your misperceptions. If you choose to *ask* the Holy Spirit, then you will *listen* to and *hear* Its voice. That is why Jesus said, "Ask and you shall receive." To ask is to choose to "tune into", to open yourself to the energetic frequency of that aspect of the One Self from which you want to receive.

To speak of your inequity, of your obvious sin, of the karma you need to work out is to gravely misperceive . To awaken spiritually is to see the perfection that you already are. Spiritual mastery does not require years of arduous spiritual practice. Mastery is simple. It requires only that you live the reality that you are right now One as God, One as Source. No principle is real or of value unless it points to The One. So, live according to this One rule; then, only the One shall rule. "Salvation comes from my one Self."[1]

Every *true* law, doctrine, religious command, moral or philosophical principle is but an extension of the rule of One—*that we are all One as Source.* Perceiving life as filled with complexity and problems, we have missed this simple truth, this short answer. Such is the way of mathematics as well: deeply complex, intricate problems may yield a single digit answer. And so it is also with the mystery of life. The answer, clear and true, underlying all the complexity of life is really just a single number: One. Oneness. We can choose to go through the process of arduous problem-solving, arduous searching or accept this truth right now. It is our choice. Only we decide how difficult or easy it will be.

We are one.

Life is one.

Me + you + every other one + everything = God

Me + you + every other one + everything + God = One.

There is nothing else to figure out. Any other answer is but a step, a fraction on its way to this eventual simplification.

You can choose to abandon your life of seeming complex problems and see there are no true problems, just a solution. This solution dissolves all fears, all guilt, all effort. When we see that as drops of water of the sea of life we hold the essence of Sea, that all the glory and power of life is already within us, we will be washed clean of multiplicity and personal struggle.

8

WHAT DO YOU THINK?

Every person and every form is but an idea in the mind of God. Each person originates from Spirit as consciousness. Consciousness begets energy. Energy begets thought. Thought takes form. Although we perceive our bodies to be separate from one another, we are all just different forms projected from the same universal consciousness. Because of this, we are not static, not inflexible person-boxes, but can change with a change of thought.

Who we think we are right now is one tiny idea in our Collective Mind. The only fixed and common point of our individual and collective being is Spirit which is evidenced as *consciousness Itself*. Everything else that we are will change. All forms change. But the I Am remains. Beyond this constant, we can think and therefore be anything we dream of. It is only our own thoughts that can ever hold us back.

Our life is simply the sum of our thoughts. If you thought exactly like the Buddha, you would be the Buddha. If you thought exactly like Jesus, you would be Jesus. Because we are all each part of everyone and everything, all is always available to us through the attraction of our thoughts. If you spent your whole life studying and imitating the thoughts of another person, you would eventually embody much of their energy— you would be a more evident part of their being and they a part of yours. It doesn't require a lifetime for that to happen. Indeed, it happens to some degree with every person that you agree with, make friends with, or that you influence. For it is not our bodies which keep us separate from each other but our thoughts.

We define ourselves by the thoughts we agree with about ourselves. Those we don't identify with, we leave behind and label as belonging to someone else. Different thoughts are made up of different energies, and by either adopting or disowning them, we establish how we will experience ourselves. Your experience of yourself is a compilation of ideas which shifts everyday according to your choices. You can confirm this by noting your self-image from one day to another.

Who you think you are is a very limited concept based upon those ideas you *currently* adhere to. When you change your ideas of who you are, your self-perception changes, and that's how you become a different person. In another moment, a week, or 60 years from now, there could be an altogether different you. This is even true physically, for what are atoms but forms resulting from thoughts?

You may no longer believe the words you wrote when a child, but does that mean that you did not write them?

What if you see a car today and say, "Oh, I like that car. Too bad it isn't mine." Two years later you may buy that very car. So from another perspective, it really *is* your car. When you practice seeing without the boundary of time, everything changes.

This is not hard to understand. However, if we apply this to the present, we can see that right now we are simultaneously alive in every single other person that exists. For each being is but another idea expressed by our One Self. Let us remember this the next time we are quick to judge another. For all we know, they could be our past or future self. Which aspect of your self do you think has written this book? Is it your past, your present, or your future?

It is your history, if you feel beyond it.

It is your future, if you feel behind.

It is your present, if you accept it.

Being everything, you see that all you desire to attain, achieve, or acquire is already within you. You simply need to call it forth into your life. Everything is possible for those who know that all possibilities exist within them.

You can select your very next moment from infinite possibilities. This is true for everyone. That is why role models—among them spiritual masters—are so important. They provide examples of different ways of thinking and what their thoughts produce in their life. That is why we look to them—to show us a way to be how they are, to get what they have. That is why we are so interested in knowing the thoughts of those we admire—to see the connection between what they think and what they do and have. Intuitively we know there is a causal relationship between them.

What you observe as the outer life of another is but the result of their own personal creation, which stems from their composite thought frequencies. What you see are their perceptions of their world in action—the manifestation of their thoughts. That is what your life is too—the experience born of the sum and characteristic energies of all your thoughts. That is why if you want to become the best athlete you can be, have the necessary physical capability, and have the opportunity to observe a master of the sport, do not study only the details of their personal and training habits. For even if you were to copy their habits exactly, you may only end up injured. Their athletic accomplishments are not brought about primarily by their practices, but by their perspective. If you could also imitate exactly how they think and their intuitive "knowing", you would be able to imitate their success.

Whatever you want to do, find someone who exemplifies it and take your cue from their thinking. If you want to bake a cake, for example, find a fine baker. Observe him, question him, read his special recipe, and listen to his insightful thoughts on the art of cake making.

It is easy to understand why spiritual seekers value the presence and teachings of a spiritual master. No matter what religion or spiritual tradition attracts you, Jesus remains one of the great masters. Hindus, Buddhists, Muslims and many others agree that He gave us an extraordinary example to live by. He came to Earth to demonstrate a particular way of life. He saw that even though the world of flesh can be dark and corrupt, although suffering was widespread and belief in separation ever present, in essence all of us are divine. We are of the same Source: we have the same "Father". Jesus saw His genuine, His immutable holiness, and He saw the same Self in all of us—men, women, leper, pauper, prostitute and priest.

It is our thoughts that merge us, and our thoughts that make us who we are. To be like Jesus, we must learn to think like Him. Read his words. Feel their essence. To be like God, think like God. If you were to match exactly the mind of the Creator, you would instantly embody the Source of All That Is. This is what Jesus did when He walked the Earth. He allowed his mind to open to and merge with the Cosmic Mind. He embodied God on Earth. So "May the mind be in you that is in Christ Jesus." (Philippians 2:5)

This is not only possible but also inevitable. We cannot help but be exactly like God. We are already the fullness of the Creator. If we do not experience this, it is because we have severed ourselves from unconditionally loving ourselves and all around us. The moment this feeling is recaptured, simultaneously we experience the presence of God—as us. For love is the only thought of God. That is why *A Course In Miracles* tells us to "Teach only love, for that is what you are." 2 Every moment we express unconditional love, that is what we are. This is what we have been practicing to do all of our life times—to be love, to be divine presence. God, the expression of unconditional love, is the supreme role model of the universe.

Our spiritual journey is directed towards God, towards our Source. We all are striving to be like God. This is not blasphemous or egotistical, but honest. It is evidence that we are wanting to remember our divinity.

Even the ego wants to be like God. However, because it sees itself as being separate from others, its existence threatened and therefore in need of being defended, it remains separate and cut off from Source. The grandiose ego also wants to be the creator of its world, but it is fear-driven, not love-driven. As such, it creates a reality that evokes only fear and resulting pain.

Subconsciously we are all trying to be the creator of our world. Are you trying to do this from love or from fear? How is your choice causing you to act? Are you controlling, judgemental, ambivalent, accepting, empowered, peaceful?

Everything aligns with Source through its perceived relationship with Source. Wherever you feel you have come from, that is where you are going. If you believe you come from a wrathful, judgmental God separate from yourself, you will become a source of fear to yourself and to others. If you feel you are simply the product of your biological parents, you are destined to live much the same way they did. If you believe you have been born of blissful love, that is what you will grow into.

This is why our relationship with our parents is of such importance in understanding life. It is a clear, human model of our relationship with our Source. During our formative years, we see our parents as being our source and define ourselves through the quality of our relationship with them. When we grow up and redefine our Source as being of a spiritual nature, we must heal any discord we feel towards our parents, lest it taint the way we continue to relate to the world.

It is not only our parents to whom we give power to

shape our lives. Any time we give another person or situation the responsibility for creating part of our life experience, we unconsciously accept them to be our source. Our energy then inevitably aligns with their energy and the qualities they embody. So if there is any person or situation that you feel is creating your world for you, examine how you see them, for that is what you are in the process of becoming. This is why is it essential that you see no other way to the Source save through your self. No one comes to the Father, except through the I Am. For a way that is not through your own self leads to a false source, not to your true spiritual home. Our relationship to Source is, in essence, eternal and unchanging. However, how we *perceive* our connection to our Source can change; then, our energetic association with it shifts accordingly. Where do you think you came from? Were you born in original sin or in creative ecstasy? Are you a victim of circumstance, life's impartial participant, or its creator? Your beliefs colour every aspect of your life.

Separation is not inherent in life. It is learned. Perception is the only basis for division in the world. How you perceive your world is how you will receive your world. Your ability to adjust your perception of the world is how you can experience a different reality. If you choose to see unity through the eyes of unconditional love, fear, with its barriers, will dissolve.

Remember that you, Jesus, the Buddha, Mother Teresa, and all beings and things are but different points of focus we hold in our Oneness. You are as much a part of Jesus or Lao Tzu as you choose to see, and likewise, they are part of you. The national hero is just another of the infinite number of lives that you are living as the great One Self that I Am. There are beings whose energy is akin to yours, but essentially every life is one of your own. Each one influences you, just as you influence it. Your brother Don is one aspect of your self, your neighbour is another of your lives as Spirit, and every person who has or will live is but another focus, perspective, and expression of the Oneness that I Am.

We experience life because we are conscious. We, as individual facets or expressions of the One Self, can choose to be conscious of different things, but we share in the same consciousness. There are no boundaries which separate us in this. There is only the one unified field of awareness.

The only significant difference between you and Jesus, between you and Sai Baba or the Buddha is that they remembered Who They Are. The only difference between you and any other is your *thoughts* about who you are. For who you are is what you think you are.

What you think about is who you are.

What *do* you think?

This is the question upon which all else rests.

All is One as God.

God is the Source of and the sum of all life.

God is the part and the whole.

God is the perfect harmony of all.

And always, God is Love.

To live in love with the world is to live as God.

Be Love, and you be God.

Be compassionate, patient, and accepting of your self and others.

Be good to each other.

Be God to each other.

The way to achieve spiritual enlightenment is not complex, obscure, or mysterious. Time, special gifts, or difficult practices are not required to achieve it, nor a handbook, a knowledge of metaphysics or adherence to a particular religious belief system. You need only think as if we are One. Do as if we are One. The path to Love is not steep and long. It is straight up and requires just one jump of perception.

For the way is truly straight and narrow.

Indeed, it can accommodate only One.

It fits only the Oneness.

So if your focus is on the One, you shall be It.

If thine eye be single, then thine "I" shall be One.
"The light of the body is in the eye. If therefore thine eye be single, then thy whole body shall be full of light." (Matthew 6:22)

9

THE PLAN

A plan of creation is not set in stone. It is just that—a plan to create, a decision to freely experience endless possibilities. The current human need for security cannot be found in the world of form, for the physical world is not static. It changes as it agrees with our thoughts about it. We create it in our self-image and can change our creations at will. The act of creating is the only constant, and it is by this divine act that we come to know ourselves as one with God.

Why worry about anything when you have the power to create your reality? "But I'm living on the street and didn't have a meal yesterday. How can you expect me not to worry?" It is worry itself which prevents the meal from coming. Doubt and fear come between you and your intentions, your desires. Do you feel worthy enough to partake of the meal which is ready just around the corner? Do you trust enough to look for it? Energy attracts similar energy: fear breeds fear; worry creates more to worry about; worthiness creates abundance. You can respond to lack or to emotional pain with trust—trust in your self to create desirable, positive outcomes.

Take no thought for tomorrow. If you feel you *must* plan, plan for the unexpected, for the universe will be a different place tomorrow—and so will you. Change is built into the very act of creating. The cosmos is created by thought, and the I Am is the Thinker, is the Cosmic Author.

We already know how the story begins and ends. As the Author, the One Self, We simultaneously knew the ending and beginning. However, the story is experienced as real for us, for these are the parts of us that we sent into what we call our world, where time and space are experienced as real, to play out Our story. Having assigned scripts and personalities to the characters, we released them into the flow of creativity, knowing where they will ultimately end up. When the story is over, every character and detail will be revealed to be simply part of the creative expression of the author—the Creator that is All.

Once Our story is over, we can decide to experience it again, edit it, switch roles, and add different sub-plots. We can do this again and again, even several million times, keeping the same general theme but developing different potentials each time, delighting in re-experiencing the endless possibilities and facets of our One Self.

The purpose of this cosmic story is to awaken to the fact that we are actually the One Creator of it all. We discover this not through playing roles and taking action but when we fall into the empty, still place between the observed and the one who observes, between the experience and the one who experiences. It is here that the reality of the Cosmic Author is found, for it is here where we are able to dis-identify with form and feel our creative essence which is behind and beyond all forms.

When we know that each of us is the author of our individual and collective experiences, how can we not rest in the lap of trust? Fate and karma dissolve in the awareness and use of our creative free will because we truly know that we create all of our experiences.

What parents do you feel will best support what you want to experience in this lifetime? Do you want to experience a boring desk job and sore hip? Do you want to create a life of joy, beauty, and abundance? Are you tired of being a victim in life's drama? Do you want to switch roles? Are you tired of just acting the part of a character and want to be the director now?

The glorious truth is that the individualized expression of the One Self you experience as "you" is the author and the protagonist in your current life drama. So too on the collective level, every facet, expression, character of the One Self is the author of the collective consensus experience.

Does this evoke fear or fill you with peace? Does this responsibility frighten or excite you? Are you ready to own your creative power?

10

JUST PERFECT

"Be ye perfect, as your heavenly Father is perfect." (Matthew 5:48) Perfection is not a flawless state, a state when one ceases to make "mistakes", but a state where one has transcended the need to judge seeming flaws and faults. It is unconditional love and unconditional acceptance that allow us to see the perfection beyond the duality of good and bad. What we call "pain" results from our belief in separation, in the belief of the reality of the egoic self which lives in a state of perpetual fear and desire. What we call "evil" also stems from ignorance of our Oneness but is coupled with willful actions to maintain and enhance a separate self—at the expense of others. Believing in separation from the One Self, we produce on-going cycles of individual and collective winners and losers, victims and perpetrators. It is by willfully acting on our Oneness that we will bring these negative and destructive cycles to an end.

Unconditional love means to love without condition, to see only perfection—then that is what exists. The Divine One Self sees all as perfect, since it sees with the eyes of unconditional acceptance and love.

Do you love your life as it is? This is not easy: the human egoic mind has developed many stipulations on what it takes to be perfect. These conditioned beliefs keep us from seeing our perfection.

How do you respond to your life with its seeming ups and downs? Is this present moment good enough for you? Are you attentive to life and patient enough with it so that you can see the light behind the shadow, the sacred fire in the darkest experiences? Can you see your life is just perfect because you chose to create it just as it is right now? If you created a shadow, it was in order to better see your light in contrast to it. Our humanity does not interfere with our divinity: it simply makes it more evident.

Do you see love's hand in everything? *God is an all or nothing principle;* everything is pure Spirit. God *is* The Everything. How then can anything be called imperfect? If we say that something isn't good, we are saying that something isn't God. That, we know, is impossible.

But what about letting others starve? What about children who are pushed into prostituting for others' gain? How can we see perfection in light of the suffering all around us?

First, we must understand that things are not what they seem. We are always asked to see beyond the physical realm. For we don't know why certain things happen in life, nor what previous actions allowed them. Only this can be said with certainty: all things have a purpose to the soul. Certain hardships make us stronger. Sometimes a person's life we see as pitiful is here only to remind us to be grateful. Often it appears others suffer to teach a lesson to those around them. Within the context of our human existence, we cannot know the reasons for such—and we do not need to. We need only decide what meaning something has for us—now. Does apparent pain in life trigger compassion in us or fear? And what do we choose to do about it? How are we going to use this to grow our soul? That is what is far more important than the appearance itself.

If everything is ultimately good, does that include the ego too? Yes. In the wisdom of the One Self, we created the ego as a foil to our true Self to serve in and ensure our spiritual awakening. To fight the ego is therefore to fight a current aspect of self. Do not fight it. Witness it at work. See it for what it is—and go beyond it by drop-ping identification with it. Accept, yes, even love the ego for playing so well, so convincingly the role we cast it in. Then discard it like a worn out garment which is of no more use to you.

Martin Buber, Jewish philosopher and theologian, told us that there is *nothing* which cannot be made sacred.

Indeed, there is nothing which is not *already* sacred. The perfection lies in correct perception. We heal all things through our very acceptance of them as divine. Problems cease to exist if we do not see them as problems. Can this perception include a broken leg? It can if by seeing the broken leg as divine we see the hidden gift in it. If we see that there is no mistake or problem in a broken leg, just an unexpected event, an unexpected form of perfection, we open ourselves to seeing that within the whole, within the One Self, all is perfect.

What we often call misfortunes are just times when the perfection of life comes in an unexpected, undesirable way. Why judge red as bad when you wanted green or feel sad that what you sought did not arrive? We have all experienced a disappointment only to see that it was a necessary prelude to something wonderful: expected house guests call to say they can't come to stay this weekend after all; then, shortly after you hear your best friend is coming to town and now you can invite her to stay with you; you lose your key only to find the diamond ring you lost a year ago in your search for it; a date cancels out on you but you go to the party anyway where you meet the love of your life; your husband leaves you, but because of that, you find your own inner strength. Such evidence abounds.

What do you call a "mistake" if it is perfect? A step, that's all. A step somewhere we are choosing to go in our Divine Oneness. When we judge something or someone, we see them as less than perfect. Because we are one with all that is, when we judge, we judge ourselves. The result is that we see ourselves as less than perfect.

Who do we judge as perfect? God. So judging also reaffirms our belief that we are separate from God. God is indeed perfect, but God is All That Is—that includes you and your irritating neighbor down the street, the sun and the rain, a broken leg and a robust body. We can learn to be grateful for the spilled paint, to bless the seeming shortcomings of our social structure, to be calm with our children's difficulties. We show and give our love to God by loving ourselves. We love God by loving the world—as it is.

Love flows through each person like a river. The stones it washes over do not affect it, but rather enhance it with color and beauty. We are the water and the movement of it is our life. When we let go and release our fears, life flows easily, joyfully. Don't make the mistake of building a dam out of your fears to hold back the flowing water. To do this is to guarantee a stuckness, an experience of false limitation.

Appreciation is active acceptance of what is. It cancels all judgment. To appreciate our experiences is to know them as fundamentally good, divine. If you observe and appreciate even your judgments, you cancel their effects. A spiritual master makes mistakes too, but doesn't judge them as negative. To the master, every mistake is simply a point of learning, a step forward.

"So be ye perfect just as God in heaven is perfect." (Matthew 5:49)

11

THE MIDDLE WAY

All things connect in the middle. It is here that they become one. It is at the middle that opposites unite, extremes are balanced, differences are reconciled and conflicts resolved. The path to the Middle Way is a sacred path, for it leads to our center. It is in the middle, at the center of our Being, where we hold the value of everything with equal respect. Bias, prejudice, judgments of right and wrong cannot exist in the center of our Being. Here we find no opposites between good and bad, male and female, hot and cold. Instead, we realize that hot and cold are simply gradations of temperature, male and female are complementary aspects of ourselves, and good and bad are just different perspectives. Likewise, there is no you and me—only different expressions of the One.

Equanimity is key to transcending duality. And an accepting, impartial heart is the birthplace of peace. To express this in metaphor, it is at the center of the wheel of life that we find the greatest stillness and balance. The center of the wheel does not judge the individual spokes that revolve around it. The spokes are recognized as simply different expressions of our Self, emanating from the one center. The person currently opposite us on the wheel is just a reflection, a mirror. And all the others who join the One Self in the middle are different images, different facets of our One Self. Each one is needed to create the perfect balance we find at the middle. The axle is the joining point; it supports and holds together the revolving spokes but is never itself changed by them.

It is impossible for the thinking mind to grasp the essence of the Middle Way. We must look with our heart. The mind tells us we have to make choices—but choices by nature reduce, limit, distort the whole. As we move into specialization in order to "stand out", we fragment ourselves, limit ourselves with labels and definitions. In this way, we lose touch with our universality, limitlessness, and infinite potential. If we feel we have to make a choice, let us choose All. Let us choose inclusiveness—the Way of the Middle.

Of course this does not mean that we do not make practical choices in our lives. We choose to go on to college instead of taking an immediate job, oatmeal for breakfast instead of toast, a walk instead of a movie, and to marry Tom not Peter. But in choosing—even in such practical matters—let us not reject entirely what we currently decided against for our well-being. Within the One, everything has value; everything has a place and purpose.

We can choose to reside in the Middle, the center—to be simultaneously connected to and detached from the whirling world. This is how we can be in this world but not *of* it. We can choose to move our attention away from residing on the rim of the wheel of life, running continuously through changing terrains, to its center where we experience stability and calm. We intuitively know that in challenging times we need to "get centered", to gather ourselves back from the superficial borders of life and connect again to our soul—the essence of our Being.

The wheel of life is always in motion, going through different fields—snow and grass, manure and daisies. If we identify solely with the edges of the wheel, always interfacing variously with happiness or sadness, always anxiously reaching and racing towards the next thing, how can we be at peace? At the surface of the wheel, ups and downs with accompanying insecurities are experienced, but at the center we find stability.

So let us choose to reside at the center of the wheel of life, watching life's events spin around us, embracing it all—supporting, loving, accepting, connected yet detached from the "drama", creative yet not controlling. It is in the center of our being that we meet the One Self. It is here we see we are not different, not separate from each other. It takes all of us: it takes the One Self to form the center. The center is where we, as infinite "spokes" of the One Consciousness, find community.

Here we find Self-love.

Here, nothing is wrong.

Hear: nothing is wrong.

And no one thing is without value.

Apathy does not exist at the center of the wheel of life. What we do find here is compassionate detachment. Our heart center continuously extends itself through positive intent and action. A detached master is not idle, just not attached to outcomes. Realizing our Oneness, the master still chooses to make a difference in the lives of others. A master is simultaneously fixed and grounded while extending his hands to the very edge of the wheel to support it and help ease its pressure.

12

LOVING EACH OTHER

May I love my beloved as God.
May I love each person as my beloved.
May I love the whole world as God.
May I love the whole world as my beloved.

Most of mankind has been under the delusion that there are many kinds of love, each different in some way from the others. We talk of parental love, romantic love, platonic love, love of neighbor, love of God. Yet these are but different expressions of the same love moving through us. It is the same love that flows out of our being. It is the same heart that receives. In the end, it is just God loving another part of Itself.

A sacred partnership is not an end in itself. It is meant to liberate—not limit—our love. It is sacred because it provides a human vehicle for the experience and expansion of love.

Although we naturally become closer to a beloved as we expand spiritually, the primary purpose of human love is to grow ever closer to our essential, unlimited Self. A relation—*ship* can be likened to a transport vessel. The vessel is simply the means of connecting the two shores. The boat itself is useful, but if we focus only on it, we miss the expansive view.

Intimacy with another is to help us grow beyond our own current perceptions of where love can and cannot exist. To love one person exclusively is not the heart's goal. Indeed, we cannot grow in authentic love for one person without growing in love for all of humanity. The heart's truest expression is unconditional love.

The sacred connection of hearts goes beyond sex and the emotional fervor associated with what we have come to call romantic love with its insecure needs and clinging. We are here to learn how to express love for all persons and things, not to focus it solely upon one or several objects of our affection.

We don't need to search desperately for a soul mate, life partner, or twin flame. We are not missing any parts, and no *body* can offer fulfillment. Love is already complete within itself. Love sees its beloved in every person. Love's very nature is to embrace others. Love cannot be confined. It consumes, it takes in all it touches. It burns away all separation, leaving only Oneness. When you truly love someone, that love expands to include the many, and eventually to include All That Is. You are Spirit. Can Spirit love only one person? Only several? Only a few hundred?

Although love transcends the personal, this does not mean you will not have one special relationship, preferring the company of one above others. And when your love expands, it does not mean that you don't love your partner. Do not confuse sexual exclusivity or monogamy with spiritual intimacy. They may or may not go hand in hand. They may be part of a love relationship—or not. A celibate monk could be your most intimate friend and your sexual partner like a remote stranger.

Although a partner is not necessary for spiritual growth, a partner can be of great assistance in this process. Your beloved can serve as your mirror, for they will not hesitate—out of unconditional love—to show you the things they see and you do not: your weaknesses, contradictions, blind spots, projections, and denials. Their teaching may come in the form of loving guidance, suggestion, feedback, bold action, and even confrontation. They will not allow you to hide the areas where you are withholding love.

True love flourishes, not because the individuals in the relationship are perfect or because the two are "ideally matched". It flourishes because the individuals have built their relationship around the adoration of Love Itself.

Relationships are sacred mirrors. In authentic love relationships, the partners mirror love to one another and by this means come to see that they are both reflections of the same Divine Light.

You have a relationship with your mother, with your neighbor, your cat, and your running shoes. You are in relationship with your car, the sun, the sea, your coffee mug, with Sam and his brother. What do these mirrors reflect back to you?

You exist in relation to others. Indeed, if there were no relationships, what is called a separate "you" would cease to exist. All that would remain would be Oneness—which is God. Ironically, that is exactly the purpose and destination of every relationship: to lead us to the awareness of unity, to the awareness of the One Self. When you feel you have merged with another person, you have effectively transcended duality. In this way, our lover can be our gateway to God. For we come to see that it is not the persona of the beloved that we merge with, but the non-personal Oneness—the I Am.

Love is not a limited commodity, so why open the floodgate of your love for just one or a few people when you can open it to all? We start by loving another, then move to living intimately with All That Is. The practice of intimacy is so holy because it is how we practice living as God. We become intimate with All That Is. Is there something beyond being intimate with God? Yes, complete unity. It is here where relationships dissolve into the nameless One. The many have then again become One. The separation is healed.

13

IMMEDIATE INTIMACY

There is only one thing that truly matters—are you expressing love right now? Love legitimizes all. When you love, you declare your true nature.

The fabric of your very existence, the substance of your soul, the stuff of atoms and of the entire cosmos is love. Yes, love helps you on your human journey. Yes, love brings harmony to your relationships. But most importantly, it is when you are loving that you most beautifully express your God essence. When you love, you live as God—you live God into our world.

You don't need to nor can you ever *get* love. You only need to express it. And it is not love when you give in order to receive something you desire or to accumulate good karma. The reason you need to express love is that when you love, the finer energy vibration that is released is the expression of your true self. By extending love, you come to know your true self—beyond the limitation of form and more encompassing than anything you can think or imagine you are.

Love *moves* us. Only steps taken in love move us forward. All else is but a stationary dance. We get many opportunities, perhaps even many lifetimes to learn to love unconditionally—to express the Self that we are. We are here to learn how to love every experience, every thing, every person, and every moment fully.

We cannot truly love without experiencing our Oneness. And to help us learn how to truly love, we can start
by being intimate with All That Is, meaning *acting* on
our Oneness with whatever is present—living that unity
by loving whatever is, and opening our heart to its gifts.
*Our Oneness is our reality. But we need to act on this reali-
ty in order to experience it. This is how we break through the
illusion of separation.*

Let our prayer be for Immediate Intimacy. May we be
able to feel our Oneness and the reality of our love
essence in every moment, with every person, every
thing, every experience.

Immediate Intimacy involves embracing every person,
situation, and experience without the weight of our conditioned past, our personal baggage. It means setting
judgments aside and relating to others without fear,
without the need to be stronger or better than others or
to control the encounter. It means meeting another and

whatever the present moment brings without needs or limitations of any kind.

Let us be open, vulnerable, and unconditionally accepting of every part of the One Self. Let us greet everyone and everything with a willingness to love in whatever way feels highest. That is how we express our God Self on earth. It is our reason for human existence.

If we cannot greet another with authentic openness, we limit the love that can be expressed. If we cannot be intimate with the many forms of our One Self, we cannot know our many faces. Let us be open to loving the stranger with the same intensity and delight we would have when meeting our long-lost brother, for he *is* our long-lost brother. Lost because we thought he was a stranger, found because we now remember our connectedness.

The eyes are a wonderful avenue to experiencing Immediate Intimacy. They can express authentic love more clearly than any words. Eye to eye, you can suddenly be intimate with a stranger. Eye to eye, your masks fall away. Eye to eye, your "I" meets their "I". When you look, truly look deeply into the eyes of another, you see your Self looking back at you. In authentic encounter, you are as one presence.

When you talk to another, you talk to God, for there is only one of us here. The Father within us is the I behind every eye.

14

WHAT DO YOU WANT?

What do you want in life? And who or what do you suppose is giving or not giving it to you? More than anything, don't we want to be free of "need"—mental, emotional, physical, spiritual? When we are not needy, we are free to fully partake in the joy of life; we are more easily able to be completely present and respond according to the need of the moment.

If you *knew* you already had everything because you *are* already everything, would you not act differently than you do now? Would you worry about tomorrow? Would you still be afraid to trust your brother? Who could be an enemy?

If you accept that God is omnipresent and therefore you are one with God simply because you exist; if you accept that God is the omnipotent creative force of the universe, and being one with God you share this same creative power, does this not mean that you already have everything because you *are* everything? If you accept your God Self, you will realize that you have no real needs. With free will that is exercised at the time of creation, you can choose at any time what you want to experience. Is this not how God lives? Have we have forgotten how to truly live because we have forgotten how God lives? Yes. Forgetfulness set it with early childhood conditioning, and so now we need to relearn, to remember how to live as our God Self.

The world tells us that external factors dictate our lives: what we have and cannot have, what we do and cannot do, whether we live or die. The world tells us we are tragically limited, can't take care of ourselves, and need to protect ourselves from others who want what we have. The world believes in our separation, not in our Oneness.

If we are each the Creator, how do we actually create? In truth, to live is to create. There is never a time when we are not creating. The energetic blue-print of every thought, emotion, action, and breath we emit returns to us in kind. What if we lived this awareness each moment? Would we not be empowered? Would we not carefully choose our thoughts, feelings, and actions, ensuring that we are creating what it is our conscious will to create?

Most of us are unconscious of our creative nature and therefore create unconsciously. When we create unconsciously, most of what we create is repetitious. It comes from our conditioned past and is therefore not the most appropriate for the fresh and new immediate moment.

To create consciously requires that you focus your creative power. You can never become more powerful than you already are. You can only become more focused, more intentional in your creating. This is why thinking is so important. Thoughts form the lens through which creative energy passes and is transformed. Thoughts color, guide, divert, shape, organize the formless creative energy ever flowing from our Being. Thoughts also evoke our feelings which further energize them. This is why it is important to be the master of your thoughts. As you think, so you will experience.

You are a unique energy formation taking the dense form of a human body. Always, the facet of our One Self known to you as "you" is connected to and broadcasting to All That Is. Everything you give, you give unto your One Self. Everything you receive, you receive from your One Self. But since energy is ever creative, what you send out as a loving wish for a friend may come back to you as a gifted bouquet of roses; similar energies join it and the result is it takes a different form. The act of creation is not linear or predictable. It is not limited by time and space. With deep love, you can sow a mustard seed in one field and reap a harvest of the finest grapes in another.

To create intentionally means to make conscious choices of what you want to create and to take the responsibility for your creations. Do you choose to see this creative power as a burden or a blessing? Choose. You can choose to make a cake, to create a new life, build a pyramid, or move a mountain. These differ only in your focus and your belief in the power of your creative capacity.

You can choose illness and pain if you like. Then when you have had enough of these, you can choose health and joy. Choose to love and watch how peace follows. Choose to worry and see how it brings pain. Each moment holds infinite possibilities and only awaits your call into your experience. It is of no grave importance what you choose. What is important is that your act of choosing helps you become aware of your identity as a creator. Evidence that you are one with God is the evidence that you can choose. For to choose is to create. And to create is to be living as God.

The mind asks, "Well, how can all of us be creators? Wouldn't this mean conflict, competition, chaos? How can each of us be gods? Spirit answers: "We are not all gods. We are all God. There cannot be more than one God."

Since there is only one God, any facet of the one God can only act with the agreement and support of the one God. Within the One Self, there is only complete agreement, complete harmony. In this way, we see that our personal choices *must* be the perfect will of God, that our choices *are* God's choices.

In the grander scheme, everything, regardless of the imperfections we seem to be creating, are just perfect. Within the One Self, everything finds agreement and is honoured and celebrated. Keep this in mind the next time you try to fix someone's life. You are not responsible for creating another person's reality, so why carry the burden of trying to do so? All you can do for another is demonstrate what it is like to be conscious of your agreement with the One Self and trust that they will come to the same realization.

All that exists is part of God and must exercise free will. Our freedom to choose reveals that we are God. The direction of those choices reveals how we are choosing to create. This becomes evident when we make choices consciously—when we truly know that the choice is ours. Not one thing in life has been sent to you by a force outside of yourself. To think otherwise is to disown your power, to seemingly give it away to family, employer, circumstances, your body, to forces that you pretend govern your life—and even to God if you believe God is outside of you.

Behind every eye is the I Am. Each of us contains Source. Truly, you cannot give your power away to another. Nor does another need it. Another person, even if he or she is very close to you, has no power to influence your life except when you choose to be one with them by choosing to hold concurrent thoughts or feelings. You don't need another person or persons to achieve your creative desires. Since you are one with All That Is, the entire universe shifts to accommodate your wishes. Did God have to ask someone for light? No, We simply declared that it be so. We created it. Pure and simple. Writer and Unity Minister Eric Butterworth saw this clearly when he said, "...We do not pray *to* God, we pray *from* the consciousness *of* God. [4]

The universal energy exists to support your creative choices, regardless of what they are. Yes, even choices that you deny having made because your conscious mind says they are not welcome. These seemingly negative "surprises" come from some level of your subconscious. Trust that you brought them into your experience in order to grow in spiritual awareness.

Mary says she wants to get married and actively pursues meeting the right person. However, whenever she does meet a wonderful man who returns her affection, she slowly loses interest in him, finding faults to justify her leaving the relationship. What is controlling Mary is her unconscious fear that if she does get really attached to a man, he will leave her just like her father did when she was four. Because as a little girl she couldn't bear her father leaving her, abandoning her, she suppressed this pain, but it has been living in her sub-conscious and has been influencing her life ever since.

Bob says he is looking for a more challenging job, but whenever he gets a better job offer, he finds some reason why he should turn it down. Subconsciously he feels he doesn't deserve to have his needs met since even his mother who loved him was not able to do this for him. In these situations there are sub-conscious factors at work which win the day, so to speak, which have been laid down by early life traumas that were not dealt with at the time. So these belief patterns live on and continue to act in the creative energy of their minds.

It is understandable, of course, to ask, "If our sub-conscious is often in control, how can we exercise free choice when it comes to creating our life experiences?" It is true that we created the sub-conscious mind as a repository for all that we could not consciously handle at the time. This includes mainly our fears which continue to exist until we are able to embrace them at the conscious level. We *can* choose, however, to bring consciousness to the fear as it surfaces and reveals itself in the present. This is the gift of the failed relationship, the loss of the job, or of an unexpected illness—it stirs up old, repressed negativity so that we can finally deal with it. When we do this, when we face our fear and hold it in the truth of our life as it exists *now*, we will almost always see that the fear is no longer valid, that it is based on some very old hurt.

When we are able to abide fully in the present moment, enter our experience without judgment, and notice the thoughts and feelings that were previously pushed away, we will see that they no longer serve us. When, being evoked by some current trigger in our life they bubble up to our conscious mind, that is the moment of the gift—when we can say, "Yes, there is an unpleasant, painful feeling which comes from a fear that I choose to no longer believe in." We may then have the strength to laugh at our fears, which is an act of such love that any darkness is washed away and all hidden faces become clear. That conscious moment is the light that dissolves that limitation. This is how we reclaim our lives.

Much of what rests in the subconscious comes from held fears—even from past incarnations—that the subconscious perpetuates in order to "protect" us from earlier experienced negativity. But as adults knowing our divine, unlimited nature, we no longer need this "protection" and can choose to release the subconscious from its role by inviting it to bring up all that it holds for our now *conscious* response and release. We may need to do this again and again until the wounded, frightened part of our self trusts that is it safe to release the old trapped energy.

Eventually, when we are able to sustain a constant awareness of our true selves, there will be no more hidden thoughts, no more psychological fear, no more subconscious mind. Then, even the super-conscious, which in this context is the unlimited, all-knowing mind of the One Self, ceases to be separate. That is what it means to be a fully realized being: all aspects of self are integrated, whole, united. The trinity of self becomes the One.

The well-known story of Aladdin and his magic lamp suggests a deep truth: that the genie we set free is really our own "magical" creative spirit which is awakened through our attention to it. When you awaken to the Spirit within you, you realize that *you* hold the "magic" of creating your heart's desires.

How *do* we create? Remember that love is the creative force behind and in All That Is. Make a choice with loving intent and imagine it complete and as if it is already so. Then, give life essence to this by filling its image with the *feeling* of love. Be grateful then, and let it go. Your faith in it will make it soar like a hot air balloon in a cold evening sky. But if a partial fear of receiving your desire is entertained—if you have even a bit of a doubt—there is a chance the balloon won't lift off the ground.

So what *do* you want? Think about this until the answer is clear. Then continue to think about it. Keep the faith balloon in the air. Do not allow the flame of your desire to waiver. Allow no diversionary wind to take you off track. Evidence of your ability to create will come and when it does, you will live with the awareness that indeed you are Spirit in human form.

You are living God.

Living is being God.

God is living you.

Your life is God, being.

Every human fear results from the belief that we are separate from God. That is why at the core of a sense of lack is the painful thought that this must indicate that we are not one with Source. The true gift of experiencing abundance is that it attests to our ability to create, to our Oneness with the Creator.

Unfortunately, our attempts to create may take us in the wrong direction. We think that creating abundance of any kind has to do with how hard we work, how much we serve, how "good" we are, how smart, healthy, good looking we are, and even how rich we already are.

Most of us repeatedly do and buy things in an attempt to improve our lives. In order to compensate for our assumed inability to create on our own, we work towards building up and hoarding more of what we think will make us feel happy, safe, and secure. Yet there is a part of us that is crying, "When am I ever going to be happy with what I have got? When am I going to have enough?" The egoic mind may respond by saying something like, "When you have a family, own your own home, and have plenty of money in the bank." Deep within, you know this is not a satisfactory answer and so you say, "But why can't I have what I want *now*? The mind says, "Simply because you don't have much at all right now." In time, however, the inner genie will surely awaken, and when it does will declare, "I can have it all because now I realize I am It All."

15

THE ATONEMENT

The perception of separation from God occurs as soon as there is the slightest notion of time and space. With the belief in time and space comes distance which separates one from another. When we see ourselves as separate beings, the concept of being more or less appears, and this is where fear and need are born. We cannot return to God because we never left God. We only had a *thought* that we did.

Separation between you and God is as real as you think it is. Being with God involves a change of attitude, not a return. Paradoxically, our effort to move back into God reinforces the illusion of separation (God is there, I am here). You cannot move in time and space *back into* God. You can only move *as* God.

We cannot change the truth by thinking it is not so. We cannot change God. We can only choose to believe the illusion of non-truth. But why would we want to believe in the illusion of separation if we are already God? As God we know we are absolutely safe, that all is well. Perhaps we chose to see ourselves as split from our One Self in playful curiosity to find out what it would be like to not feel like we were God. Perhaps we chose to see ourselves as separate simply to have the experience of joyfully reuniting in Oneness again. Could it be that the sweetness of that embrace is so compelling that we create the pain of believed separation just so that we can experience the elation of atonement? Have we chosen all the bumps we experience in life simply to make our reunion even more glorious? Perhaps we chose to experience this world with its pain so that we could grow in wisdom and compassion not possible if we never forgot our unity. Perhaps in the infinite wisdom of the One, we left home in order to experience again what home truly *is*. The irony is that we return by remembering that we never could nor did we ever leave our home in God in the first place.

16

ALL RIGHT NOW

God's domain is right here, right now. Everything exists in reality and potential in the now. You can only be conscious of anything *now*.

The now does not move. Linear time is illusory. In this context, time is best understood as being vertical, not horizontal, holding every potential simultaneous in the now, awaiting our decision as to what we want to experience. Any belief that we cannot experience something is the mind's limitation, not of the One Self. And we can choose to experience the same things as many times as we wish.

All is right Now.

Right Now is All.

Now is All Right.

God is, and we are, All Right Now.

When we live as the One Self in this perpetual now moment, we dispel the illusion of space and time and therefore of separation. And it takes no time to do this. "It has taken time to misguide you so completely, but it takes no time at all to be what you are."⁵ Our One Self exists now and awaits only our decision to experience it. To the linear thinking mind, the explosion of creation into unlimited forms and the re-union with Source has already taken millions of years and still requires more time. All of this, however, must be God's choice to delve into that flash explosion so that every possible facet of the One Self can be appreciated, savored, and glorified.

As God we choose to experience the intricacies of every snowflake that falls and the beauty of every sunrise. We choose to explore and relish every part of us: every flutter of our wing, every grain of sand, every human birth—through all of eternity. We even choose to experience our dark side, to experience ourselves cut off from God—devoid of love and hope.

We want to miss nothing. That is why we created the illusion of time, for it allows us to enter the unlimited now and explore the One Self—even in the illusion of separation—for as long as we choose.

Can you imagine how incredible it would be if you could shrink and divide yourself so that you could see and feel every cell and every atom in your body? Imagine experiencing just one moment of every aspect of your biology. After such an experience, how much more would you appreciate the unfathomable glory of doing this for one whole day?

In this context, each person can be likened to a cell of God's body, being experienced and appreciated by the entire mind of God. We experience life in this apparent stream of time, although all has actually taken no more than an instant in the mind of the God. This we do to appreciate our One Self fully and bring the love that we are to each and every aspect of our Self. In this way, the

One experiences the beauty of the many so that the many can experience the glory of the One.

The One Self exists so it can meet the many and the many can meet the One. Diversity and Oneness. Diversity in Oneness. Ah, the truth of paradox.

It is right now when the diversity can collapse into simple unity, where past and future can become meaningless and effort absurd. We can right now exist as pure awareness knowing there is only the now and that there is only one life—and it is Us. You may have already had a glimpse of this reality—when time stops and your sense perceptions expand. It is then when you can feel your leaves brushing against your branches and feel the wind rush through your feathers. Sometimes this comes by grace, and sometimes this comes through shock, as your heart is jolted and compassion is complete. In this way, suddenly you *are* the abused wife, you *are* that beggar, that maimed soldier, that starving infant. It is then when you experience the "other" as the "self". Any time this happens, this connection sings to you of a point beyond judgment and duality. And this brings clarity. In this space of connection, what needs to be done next is easy, spontaneous, and healing.

We can invite this experience into our lives by living as if we already know that we are one with all, right now. Each of us has likely had this experience, but how can we sustain it? To have something permanently, we must choose it perpetually.

Be Us, Now.

Now—Us

One moment, one Being.

Be the One Moment. Be the One Self.

Be the one Now.

Be the One, now.

Every moment embodies eternity, just as every person embodies God.

17

YOU SHALL SET FREE THE TRUTH

The human race has accumulated much mind knowledge, yet pain, conflict, and violence still prevail. What use is our knowledge if the innocent child, ignorant of the world, is closer to heaven than the most erudite scholar or priest? Learning *more* will not set us free from the limitations and travails of life.

We deceive ourselves by thinking we need to *know* more, *do* more in order to live joyfully. This self-deceit has been our excuse for maintaining our masks, pretensions, and safeguards and for denying that it is our own personal refusal to experience bliss that keeps it from us. Every limitation is self-imposed.

The truth *will* set you free, but first *you* must set free the truth—by *living* it!

Freedom does not come from teleporting, manifesting out of thin air, or flying. Neither is it acquired by having extensive knowledge of the spiritual realms. It is by living detached from the cares, worries, and fears of this world that we come into our authentic selves and experience the reality of our freedom. Simply allowing things to be will reveal the inherent divinity in all of life. So will consciously letting go of fears and surrendering to the effortless flow of life in unplanned and non-judgmental living within the present moment. We need to take the risk of being vulnerable, of dropping our defenses to experience the truth of our Being. We need to risk opening to the perfection, to the loving benevolence of the Oneness.

When we stop working so hard to maintain the illusion of our separation, the reality of the One Self will be obvious. The One Self is who we are as soon as we stop pretending to be otherwise. When the mind asks, "What is God?" the heart points to whatever is present and says, "This." God is what *Is*. "I Am that I Am." God is not out there, but here.

It is not with the mind but with the eyes of innocence that we become aware of this truth. Innocence is a state in which we are open to the experience of truth. It is the unclouded perception of what is.

It is the limited thinking mind that hides our innocence. The One Self cannot be grasped by thought. Thought, by its very nature, isolates one thing from the whole, breaks it off so to speak and therefore must be false or a distortion at best. If we are still struggling spiritually by trying to find out more, may our prayer be that we come to "learn" enough so that we can understand that all our learning was not only unnecessary for spiritual awareness but an obstacle to our awakening. May spiritual truth be born out of the ashes of our knowledge.

THE NEW AVATARS

To be the Christ is simply to be awakened to our divinity and to live it fully in the world. The ancient term for this is avatar. Throughout the history of mankind, there have been only several avatars like Jesus, the Buddha, and Krishna, but now the One Self is ready for a whole portion of humanity to live their divinity in human form. As many more now start living their divinity, it will be increasingly difficult for others to ascribe their holiness to an outside God.

There is no limit to the number or restrictions on who can awaken to their divine nature. If you are reading this now, you are surely part of this potential collective.

To live from our divine nature does not mean that we give up our humanity. Jesus and the Buddha knew well the sorrows of the world. Their compassion was great because their humanity was deep.

In this time, we will not only predictably witness spiritual awakening on a larger, perhaps even a mass scale, but will likely see more females awaken spiritually out of the need to bring into balance the male-female energy polarities. More importantly perhaps is that often the new avatars will no longer be just a single person, but a pair. They will not need to be cloistered nuns, lonely hermits, or chaste gurus. Many a new avatar will be male and female couples who live very normal, very human lives and together embody a single unit of balance and wholeness. Jesus and his beloved Mary were the harbingers of the divine couples in our current age. It is their legacy and lineage we are now fulfilling. They shone as one, as the embodiment of Love, yet only He was seen. We were not yet ready at that time to see Her, to see Them. Jesus and Mary knew and accepted this. They knew they were preparing the way.

There was a time in humanity's history when females held the most power and influence. Later the power shifted to men. Now, we are healing the male-female polarity, healing this separation in the move to our Oneness. Neither male nor female will need to live in the shadow of the other. The power in their oneness will be visible.

"When two or more are gathered in My name, there I Am also." (Matthew 18:20) Any true joining attests to the Oneness that is our reality. Let us teach our Oneness by living in unity and love. For when we gather our selves together in the name of love, there the I Am presence will be.

19

LIVING GOD

We do not need the external world to change before we can find peace. We only need bring love to it to have peace. Life is love. Love is life. We start one when we chose the other. We cannot leave what we cannot love, for finding love wherever we are is exactly the reason we are here. And we don't want to leave this earth party until we get our gift.

How can we experience the benevolence of the universe unless we trust ourselves and one another? Unless we trust God? Our security cannot be found in the outer world, in anything or anyone outside of ourselves—that includes a detached outside god. The peace that comes with knowing that we live in a universe of our choosing and all is well is available to us now. The peace of God comes from knowing that we are all pieces of God.

Jesus was no more intrinsically holy than the thieves who died beside him. He differed from them, however, in his knowing that "I and the Father are One." Knowing we are all One with the Father, how *could* He judge "others"? He knew that God was equally present in everyone and had enormous compassion for those who had forgotten this. Until we remember this primary reality of all life, we cannot know what we do to each other or to our world.

It is true that you cannot love yourself until you love God. It is equally true that you cannot love God until you love yourself, since they mean the same thing. Similarly, you love God by loving your brother—as your self.

We are as important to God as God is to us. Through us does the One come to know Itself in form. Through us, God's experience of Itself is made complete. We are God experienced and expressed. We are the Living God—*living* God. The kingdom is at hand, for it is in *our* hands now. *It is within us.*

To acknowledge and celebrate the One Self is our purpose. It is what we are called to do. When we appreciate every person, thing, experience as the expression of the One Self, we abide in joy and peace, the natural state of our soul. What effort, what defenses or grievances are necessary when we abide in the safety of our unity? All needs dissolve; only grace remains.

We don't need to grasp for air: we simply need to breathe. Similarly, there is no need to grasp for God Who is omnipresent. It is by our awareness of this that we enter into a whole new dimension of peace. Let us abide in and act from this realization.

This book can never end, for in you it now lives forever.

And forever our love will expand.

Amen.

As every ending is a beginning, let us begin.

NOTES

A Course in Miracles (Foundation for Inner Peace, Glen Allen,
    California 1990) Workbook, Part I, Lesson 96, p. 167
Ibid. Text, Chapter 6, p.87
Ibid. Workbook, Part II, Lesson 307, p.443
Butterworth, Eric, *The Creative Life* (Jeremy P. Tarcher/Penguin,
    New York, NY 2001), p. 9
A Course in Miracles, Text, Chapter 15, p. 282

n   Namaste Publishing

Our Publishing Mission:
To make available publications that acknowledge, celebrate and encourage others to express their true essence and thereby come to remember Who They Really Are.

Namaste Publishing
P.O. Box 62084
Vancouver, British Columbia v6J 4A3
Canada
www.namastepublishing.com
Email: Namaste@telus.net
Tel: 604-224-3179
Fax: 604-224-3354

To place an order see www.namastepublishing.com or
E-mail: namasteproductions@shaw.ca

To schedule the author for a teaching or speaking event,
E-mail: namasteteachings@telus.net